ROOFTOP GARDENS

ROOFTOP GARDENS

THE TERRACES, CONSERVATORIES, AND BALCONIES OF NEW YORK

Denise LeFrak Calicchio and **Roberta Model Amon**
Photography by **Norman McGrath**

RIZZOLI
NEW YORK

First published in the United States of America in 2011
by Rizzoli International Publications, Inc.
300 Park Avenue South
New York, NY 10010
www.rizzoliusa.com

Editor: Philip Reeser
Designer: Victoria Pohlmann

2011 2012 2013 2014 / 10 9 8 7 6 5 4 3 2 1

Distributed in the U.S. trade by Random House, New York

Printed in China

ISBN-13: 978-0-8478-3606-2

Library of Congress Catalog Control Number: 2010941020

Contents

Foreword

by Evelyn H. Lauder

The romance of having a city garden is a love affair hard to relinquish. The contrast between the noise of the city streets and the calmness of the sky's proximity, as well as seeing breathtaking views and inhaling fragrant blossoms, keeps the affection alive.

Our romance with our rooftop garden began in 1988. When my husband, Leonard, our sons, and I first took a real look at the penthouse apartment available in our building, nothing had prepared us for the glory we witnessed 150 feet above the street. The sky was a rich blue that autumn day, and the sun was intensely bright, illuminating the view of Central Park. The terrace had been lovingly planted and cared for by the seller since the 1950s—with mature vines, many hydrangeas, rhododendrons, privet, trees, and perennials. We agreed to the purchase there and then. To this day, many of the original plantings are still in place and, of course, have been added to over the years.

Every morning, either before or after exercise, I put on a beaten-up old straw hat and grab my leather gloves and ratchet pruner to gather roses or zinnias for our breakfast table and sink top. Sometimes I even find some ripe *fraises du bois* ready for enjoyment. In summer we harvest the eggplant, zucchini, and tomatoes carefully planted by Phebe, our horticulturist. Imagine us bringing ratatouille to the country for dinner.

In autumn, Phebe plants hundreds of bulbs, which emerge in spring to thrill the soul and surprise the eye. It is then that the garden is most colorful—white from lilacs, azaleas, bridal veil bushes, and tulips; pink from the blossoms of the crabapples; lavender from the wisteria; yellow, white, and orange from narcissus. Even the blue grape hyacinths offer a contrast to the bouquet of colors. It is then that the garden comes alive again after its restful sleep.

A rooftop garden is not anything like gardening in the ground. Tree roots need yearly pruning or they will become "pot bound" in the limited space of the planter boxes. Wind and heat from the sun dry out the soil faster than they would if the plants were in "real" gardens, and consequently much more water is required.

The good news is that there are no groundhogs, squirrels, or deer to chew away at the plants.

A rooftop garden is not like any other garden in the world.

A feeling of euphoria engulfs everyone stepping out the door and over the threshold to a world of light, color, fragrance, and loveliness. Roberta Model Amon, Denise LeFrak Calicchio, and Norman McGrath have brought you over that threshold.

Introduction
Sky-High Gardens

by Dominique Browning

Who hasn't walked through the streets of New York City, craning a neck to get a glimpse of penthouse life, and wondered at the profusion of plant life sprouting and spilling down the limestone facades of the buildings? You may be walking down a street that hasn't an inch of green life on it, but you can glance skyward and see pine trees etching a line against the cerulean blue, or tall, blowsy grasses with billowing puffs of seed swaying in the breezes, or perennials throwing off sprays of riotously colorful blooms, or the pale bark of birch trees glowing in the moonlight. Life, in other words, thrives at all strata of our built world. Plants cling to skyscrapers, matching their strength against gusts of wind and hail, and caring not a whit that they defy growing zones, much less gravity. These are the stalwart residents of New York's rooftop gardens.

Most of us mere mortals have never had the chance to ride the thermals in the city's stratosphere, gazing down at the terraces below—which is why a book like this is such a treasure. We get glimpses, from street level, of tufts and sprigs and branches and anything else that overhangs. But the photographs included here send us soaring to dizzying heights. We can wander through serene gardens that evoke the Zen peacefulness of Japanese teahouses, or be buoyed by the romantic allure of English borders whose colors change through the seasons. We are introduced to fascinating ideas of what it means to make a garden and what it takes to transport the gardener: sometimes it is a piece of art—a vivid, zany sculpture—as much as a gracefully bowed tree that defines the terraced landscape. Terrace gardens come in all shapes and sizes.

Terrace gardeners must work against nature, which makes their creations all the more remarkable. It is a demanding sort of gardening. The winds that ricochet off the concrete canyons are brutally desiccating. The sunshine, pouring down all day long, burns unrelentingly. Rain is unreliable and brings down the soot of the city's furnaces and engines; and of course the soil is necessarily thin, lest the roof beneath cave in under the weight. Yet the people who plant and tend these terraces are as determinedly cosseting of them as any gardener in the oasis of a park or suburban backyard—perhaps even more so. City life can be harsh and dirty, unremittingly loud, and distracting. For those who love gardens—who need to go to the ground to create a refuge—and find respite in even the tiniest corner of nature, the rooftop garden is a treat indeed, and it is what makes the terrace gardener persevere.

There was a time in New York City when a designer dreamed of connecting a series of terrace gardens by means of parapets and bridges that would link buildings throughout midtown, starting at Rockefeller Center. That never happened, though ultimately the rooftops of some of those buildings were beautifully landscaped. One can only imagine what such a floating park might have looked like—and be amazed at the possibility. Best of all, *Rooftop Gardens* offers us a chance to leap tall buildings with the turn of a page. We share with the hawks of Central Park their bird's-eye view of the mysterious celestial treasures being tended high up in the air.

ROOFTOP GARDEN as *Sanctuary*

A respite from the trials of a busy life: a fantasy enclosure or leafy retreat

A Country Garden
High Above the City

Though the time had come to move back into the city, the owners of this apartment could not bear to totally leave behind the pleasures of country living. They patiently spent years looking at real estate until they found what they were looking for—a place that incorporated the comfort and easy sophistication of a stylish cottage surrounded by a garden, albeit in the middle of a teeming metropolis.

Visible from almost every room, the terrace garden designed by Halsted Welles Associates is approximately two thousand square feet and wraps around the apartment, affording ample space for repose and private outdoor living seldom found in New York City.

The enclosed conservatory, designed by architect Robert Stewart Burton, is a space where inside and outside delightfully converge. The space is used all year long; here, the owners grow amaryllis, paperwhite narcissus, and cyclamen during the winter months, and a camellia that the family has tended for more than five years comes into bloom every February and March.

LEFT: Blossoming dwarf crabapple trees on the east terrace line the path to the side of the building facing south. Passing through the trellised arch, one continues to another section of the garden, which wraps around the entire apartment.

Beyond the branches of fruit trees brushing against the conservatory in early spring, one can see evergreens including juniper that have weathered the winter in deep, heavy containers. After a few days of warm sun, fruit trees blossom and spring bulbs burst into flower. These are followed by snowdrop anemones, an alpine wildflower with delicate white petals. In late April arches of lattice and trellis are covered in climbing vines, completing the impression of a country garden coming into bloom.

In subsequent months the garden is enhanced by plants that are both bright and sweetly scented, including purple and white fuchsias and moonflowers. Nicotiana, sometimes called "flowering tobacco,"

BELOW: In compliance with stringent city codes related to weight of planters and furniture on a terrace, a mixture of inert material serves to lighten the weight of the soil in heavy containers planted with flowering bulbs in spring. Daffodils come early, followed soon after by peonies, lilacs, and roses.

RIGHT: The garden is visible from almost every room of the apartment, particularly the conservatory. Seen through the floor-to-ceiling glass walls, the skyscrapers serve as a backdrop to a view of the garden that changes with every season.

provides the look of carefree beauty. Honeysuckle and fragrant petunias come later, along with clematis and heliotrope. As spring gives way to summer, lilies and campanulas add their bell-like blooms to the display. At night the white flowers of viburnum seem to glow, making a perfect backdrop for outdoor meals or quiet contemplation.

OPPOSITE: The south side of the building is center stage for flowering bulbs in early spring, wisteria later on. Fruit trees, including pear and apple, thrive in the sun. Summer brings roses, as well as honeysuckle, clematis, fuchsias, and various annuals such as verbena, fragrant petunias, and heliotrope.

RIGHT: Dwarf crabapple trees tower over buildings that make up a typical urban landscape. Maple and beech trees are also planted on the terrace.

PAGES 8–9: There is great pleasure in dining out of doors in the city. The lights in neighboring buildings seem ornamental, and the presence of greenery amidst the architecture becomes particularly striking.

Echoes of Exotic Places

Overlooking an active Chelsea streetscape is a tranquil rooftop garden that appears to be carved out of the wilderness. Artifacts from Thailand, China, and Burma are displayed here, some of them partially obscured by winding branches of wisteria. The impression of spaciousness is enhanced by the fact that the garden is on three levels. Each section is set on lateral steel beams that protect the actual roof of the building. The garden's flooring is composed of eighteen-inch square pavers whose surface—uniform in texture and color, and brushed and polished to look like Tuscan stone—visually unifies the three zones of the garden.

A somewhat exotic mood is created by recessed seating areas with deep cushions and carved Indian marble lighting fixtures under pergolas composed of Indian columns covered by drooping wisteria.

The linchpin elements of the garden include royal purple wisteria, Japanese maple and styrax, weeping blue atlas cedar, daphne, cotinus, topiary junipers, and Japanese blue pines. These signature

LEFT: The dining area on the top deck is reached through two gardens on lower levels. The skylight is amidst a bed of juniper and Russian sage, while blooming variegated yucca rises boldly from a base of leafy fronds. Royal purple wisteria partially covers the pergola to make a shady corner.

specimens are complemented by a host of perennials and annuals, including gomphrena, artemisia, echinops, echinacea, terra cotta yarrow, and variegated grasses and yucca.

Though the owner, Manhattan-based interior designer Thomas Hays, scrupulously prunes the burgeoning wisteria, the intended effect is still that of free-flowing fields in a tropical locale where it is least expected.

OPPOSITE: Deep, comfortable seating under a pergola supported by Indian carved columns sets the mood of a serene place to relax. A Burmese temple gong above the sofa suggests the Far East, as does the Thai Buddha on the tabletop. A luscious cinnamon fern and two dwarf topiary pines frame the seating area.

RIGHT: From a table of etched aquamarine glass, one can enjoy open-air dining and a view of the plantings on the level below as well as urban rooftops to the north. An Indian carved-marble lighting fixture casts arabesque shadows on the table at night.

LEFT: A pyramid skylight surrounded by an abundance of delicate vines, grasses, and field flowers is the focal point of the north deck, which also provides a prelude to the dining area above. A styrax and Japanese pine frame the scene, while a dwarf topiary and royal purple wisteria give the terrace depth.

BELOW: A sense of escape from street life below is heightened by the spire of the Empire State Building in the distance. Two weeping blue atlas cedars and a trellis of Brazilian *ipe* provide a background for carved Indian columns from Rajasthan.

A Garden of Wonders

The ample gardens of this rooftop terrace, comprising 2,200 square feet with expansive views of the East River, serve as a backdrop for a great number of activities: lounging, gardening, outdoor dining, and strolling along an unexpected ornamental path.

The garden—designed by Halsted Welles Associates—has south, east, and north exposures and is used all year round. In summer, a multitude of flowers flourish in planter boxes, pots, and undulating borders. The gardeners report no particular preplanning, using only pure instinct in selecting plants that will look beautiful and do well. Each season brings its own extraordinary offering. Pansies, crocuses, daffodils, and irises in spring are followed by wisteria, peonies, roses, and blossoming fruit trees during the summer months. Come fall, chrysanthemums, asters, and cyclamen create a new palette of purples, oranges, yellows, and bronze. The view

RIGHT: Grape hyacinths and reticulated irises grow alongside flowering spring bulbs and pansies under a red maple, creating a lush background for dining out of doors in a corner of the terrace where there is a partial view of the East River.

beyond the terrace changes as wild grasses grow taller, creating a more protected feeling as the weather becomes colder. By the time snow arrives, the garden has been covered in layers of salt hay and balsam boughs to insulate whatever has a chance of surviving through the season.

A "back door" near the kitchen provides easy access to vegetables such as tomatoes, lettuces, and herbs including Greek columnar basil, which rises knee-high in large leafy bushes as early as the first week in June. The fruit garden, planted separately, offers strawberries, blueberries, raspberries, and grapes all summer long. On the west side of the terrace, away from the blazing sun, is an area the owners have designated "Jurassic Park," where oversize junglelike plants grow wildly.

OPPOSITE: The undulating path of the south terrace was intended to replicate the yellow brick road from *The Wizard of Oz.* At every turn in the path comes a surprise among the mixture of colorful annuals and perennials that change with the season and the whim of the owners and gardeners.

RIGHT: Small statuary, from a horse farm in Connecticut where the owners once lived, can be found all around the garden and lends an air of whimsy and discovery.

The well-kept secret of this garden, and others like it, is a metal liner that extends from one end of the roof to the other, covering every inch of the surface. The brick flooring of the garden is laid over the liner. Pots and planters are filled with a mixture of soil and less dense nutritive material to keep their weight to a minimum. All is done within the specifications of city codes to prevent leaks and related damage to the building.

The garden is a source of endless delight to its owners, who admit to enjoying the best of city and country life—all in midtown Manhattan.

OPPOSITE: The "secret garden" is, in the words of the owners, "for reading, sanctuary, shade, and meditation." Among the ample foliage are herbs in deep planters and in sunnier spots fresh vegetables, such as tomatoes, lettuce, and squash.

BELOW: Plantings on the terrace facing the East River frame the view and offer a remarkable contrast between nature on the terrace and river activity below.

A Cottage Garden
away from the Bustling City

Fifteen stories above the street is a rooftop terrace surrounding an English-style cottage with a dark green door. A tap of the bronze knocker brings the owner, eager to lead the way through his picturesque garden. A variety of containers and pots—placed along the outside walls of the terrace and against the cottage structure—overflow with roses, lilacs, geraniums, and peonies. Explaining the modus operandi of the horticulturalist who helped his wife and him start the garden, he says, "Rebecca Cole once declared that in a well-planted garden you do not see any bare soil." Following Cole's advice, he does not hesitate to remove plants past their prime to make room for more seasonal ones ready to bloom.

Here, where other gardens on nearby roofs create the impression of a verdant neighborhood in the sky, there is sun from the east and south almost all day and spectacular sunsets in the evening. Red maples and climbing vines create the impression of a year-round garden in the colder months.

The couple, who live in an apartment on a lower floor, purchased the rooftop retreat after fourteen years of living in the building. The catalyst for it was the husband's growing collection of treasures —miniature books and replicas of famous rooms complete with

OPPOSITE: The garden is approached by passing under an arbor covered in red mandevilla, which blooms all summer and into fall until the first frost.

BELOW: The roof structure, named "Morgan Cottage" after the wife's Welsh ancestors, serves as a retreat and accommodates the occasional guest.

hand-carved furniture—that was crowding out their living space and testing his wife's patience. The "upstairs" cottage, named "Morgan Cottage," was the perfect repository for the objects as well as the occasional guest. The garden, however, was the unanticipated bonus and has afforded the couple hours of satisfaction through their gardening efforts and relaxation while sitting amongst plants and flowers away from the bustling city below.

LEFT: Maple and birch trees provide a backdrop for a profusion of potted plants, which include lilacs, roses, peonies, petunias, and pink dianthus. By the owners' admission, they acquire whatever annuals catch their fancy in the greenmarket.

BELOW: The fan flower blooms in a shower of dainty petals for most of the summer. The Latin term for the flower's genus, *Scaevola*, means "left-handed" and refers to the hand- or fan-shaped form of the blossoms.

LEFT: When maples turn crimson, the lady of the garden is at her best. The sculpture was found for the owners by gardener Rebecca Cole.

OPPOSITE: In this urban version of an English garden, there is a general feeling of lushness. The object is not to leave a square inch of earth unplanted.

Zen Tranquility
in New York

On the roof of a four-story Manhattan town house a Japanese garden, designed and constructed by its owners, proves to be a singularly peaceful, not to mention slightly incongruous, haven in the midst of city life. The husband and wife, French and Japanese respectively, have followed to the letter the dicta of tea-ceremony gardening to create a tranquil green space.

Accommodating the footprint of the town house, the garden is forty-two feet deep and twenty feet wide and feels consistent with the intimacy and privacy of gardens in Japan. Pines, weeping cherry trees, and hemlock act as screens, blocking the surrounding cityscape. Consequently, there is nothing to disturb the serenity of the view into the garden from the bedroom.

A stone *tsukubai*, or water basin, is to the right of the platform from which one steps into the garden. Here, one may pause on the smooth river stones and ladle water from the basin to wash before going on

RIGHT: Double-bay doors open from the master bedroom onto the *engawa*, the veranda-like structure that separates the interior from the garden. The path across the mossy lawn takes multiple turns to allow specific sight lines at various points.

OPPOSITE: The water basin has running water supplied by a bamboo spout for cleansing before a tea ceremony. Beyond the basin is a glass skylight, which is surrounded by a carved bamboo border, yellow irises, and black bamboo. The skylight—with its reflective surface—suggests a pond.

BELOW: Looking toward the master bedroom from the teahouse a second skylight is visible, allowing light into the interior. Above it is a Japanese black pine clipped in a traditional Japanese style; its branches have been shaped by weighting them with hanging stones. Bordering the teahouse, blooming azalea bushes trimmed in the shape of mounds introduce a dash of color to this Asian garden.

to have tea. Further on, what appear at first to be small pools of clear water are actually skylights allowing light to the third and fourth floors below.

The garden is designed with a "middle ground" of trees and shrubs intended to create a focus two-thirds of the way into the space to make the end seem farther away than it really is. Similarly, stones that make up the walking path were placed in gradually decreasing size to lengthen the perspective and increase the sense of space.

There are four stone statues in the garden, each a representation of Buddha or Jizoo Bosatsu, and they are placed so that only one can be seen from any one point.

Following the walking stones, which have been thinly sliced to minimize weight, the visitor arrives at the teahouse. Plasticized paper in the sliding panels allows views of the garden from within. The teahouse was constructed of red cedar, from the interior space to the outside shutters and roof. The space is perfect for a small tea ceremony. A brazier lined in copper is used to warm the space in colder months. There is just enough room on the floor for two tatami, woven grass mats for sleeping.

LEFT: Inside the teahouse there is an atmosphere of serenity. The structure, built entirely of red cedar, is a haven from which one can contemplate the verdant garden outside. An openwork bamboo fence, seen at left, serves to formalize the entry to the teahouse.

RIGHT: Panels of plasticized paper create translucent windows facing the garden and offer protection from the weather so that tea ceremonies can be held throughout the year.

A City Terrace
as Interpreted by an Artist

In a neighborhood that has recently found a new identity, many former industrial buildings, as well as newly constructed residential buildings, offer refuge in gardens and on terraces well above street level. Cobbled streets are reminiscent of a time when small industries thrived in this part of town. Today, the conversion of an elevated railway to a park, the High Line, brings public and private space together in an innovative way.

From this garden, designed by artist and garden designer Paula Hayes, the High Line is partially visible through a "fence" of irregular lengths of sea-worn driftwood along the eastern edge. A path of irregularly cut paving stones set among rounded river stones leads to the back of the building where the space opens to a large area bordered by a mix of deciduous trees, evergreens, bushes, and grasses, a sampler of the many types of plants that can survive on a windblown rooftop. Some grow in enormous pots, others in silicone bags designed by Hayes, whose creative work is marked by thought-provoking combinations of natural and synthetic materials.

LEFT: On a rainy day, Paula Hayes's inventive juxtapositions are particularly evident in rough and smooth surfaces, waving grasses and solid stone paving. Soft, baglike plant containers impel us to see familiar objects differently and to consider new uses for common materials.

LEFT: Roughly cut flagstones progress from the first terrace to a larger space on the north side of the building. Slanted skylights bring natural light to the interior and illuminate the terrace with light from inside at night.

OPPOSITE: A grouping of wicker pod chairs invites guests to lounge and enjoy the open sky. A mix of evergreens approximately six feet high screens out intruding views of nearby buildings.

The path to this larger space on the building's north side incorporates oversize skylights that allow natural light to enter an art gallery and viewing room below. At night, these surfaces become pools of light that illuminate the outdoor space.

One level above is another terrace, designed specifically for outdoor dining. Tucked into the right angle of a small structure on the roof, this garden is framed by a combination of corrugated metal and a dense evergreen hedge tall enough to partially screen out urban views and create a feeling of privacy.

OPPOSITE: The corrugated metal exterior of a small structure on the rooftop creates a sheltered corner, perfect for sunbathing until the sun shifts to the west.

RIGHT: Paula Hayes's biomorphic silicone pouches gently support a plant's root-ball. The receptacles are weather-resistant and not likely to leak. Visually, they form a striking contrast with the precast pavers of the flooring and the brick wall of the building.

Luxurious Living on a Penthouse Terrace

From inside, one catches glimpses of trees and flowering plants through the windows out to the garden. One can also hear the soothing sound of water.

The L-shaped garden, designed by Halsted Welles Associates in close collaboration with the owner, is a welcoming retreat. It is simply furnished with wrought-iron chairs and plump cushions. A trickling fountain mounted to the brick chimney wall explains the sound of water. The west-facing side of the penthouse terrace is shaded and cool, a pleasant place to dine on a summer night. Large, smoky mirrors, their surfaces worn with age, suggest larger spaces beyond.

There is pleasure in watching the seasons change in this rooftop garden, which is abundantly planted with birch trees, hostas, and wild grasses. The plants—accommodated in decorative containers, urns, and planter boxes—are lush and create a feeling of intimacy.

RIGHT: A stone fountain mounted to a chimney wall trickles into a basin of floating water hyacinths. The basin is flanked by pots of elephant ear. To the left of the fountain are dragon lady holly and a Japanese flowering dogwood. These are underplanted with English ivy, liriope, and water hyssop.

While the garden is a pleasure to live in, its presence is also felt from the inside of the apartment. Visible greenery and tree branches brushing against the many windows add a sense of calm. The terrace, in addition to serving as a buffer from the outside world, is a welcoming environment to enjoy the outdoors under the sun or the moon and the stars.

OPPOSITE: Misty images in a smoky mirror suggest a gateway to another garden. Chinese lions resting on a bluestone tabletop and a terra cotta–tiled roof above the trellis add to the dreamlike impression.

BELOW: Reflections of the immediate garden and distant city are captured in a mirror that is covered in decorative metalwork with English ivy entwined in its tracery.

LEFT: The brick arch supports an interior chimney and frames the terrace dining area. Purple pansies are banked high in the planters and at the bases of crabapple trees. The dining table is made of New York bluestone. All the plant containers are faced with the same material.

OPPOSITE: A curving length of white birch rises from a base of Grand Master hosta and purple pansies, adding intrigue to a corner of the terrace hedged in boxwood.

PAGES 46–47: Structural and decorative elements come together on this spacious terrace in a pleasing combination of nature and architecture.

ROOFTOP GARDEN as *Outdoor Room*

A direct extension of the interior: outdoor living in an urban context

Outside Views from Every Room

The L-shaped terrace was created on top of an old building when an additional four stories were recently added—the new structure was set back to create the outdoor space. The result is a novel mix of old and new, created by the architectural firm SHoP and owner Jay Johnson, principal of Jed Johnson Associates. In the original plans there were no specifications for an outdoor water source or access to drains. Luckily, the owners purchased the apartment in the early stages of construction and the problem was easily remedied.

Well groomed and almost monochromatic, except for a conspicuous trimming of green from the plants, this terrace is a perfect extension of the tastefully decorated apartment. It is a visual bonus and, as one of the owners says, "You have a view of nature from everywhere in the apartment, including the shower."

OPPOSITE: Weather-seasoned teakwood chairs and tables on a terrace enlivened by birch trees and boxwood offer a green oasis in the midst of a busy urban neighborhood.

The inviting exterior space is just six floors above street level but feels far removed from the bustle of city life. "It is amazingly peaceful and serene," according to the owner, voicing the view of many urban garden-terrace owners. "The city is all around you, yet you are in this oasis of green in the midst of it all." Sturdy outdoor furnishings are made of teak scrubbed and naturally weathered to look appropriate for outdoor use. The planters constructed of *ipe* wood from Brazil can withstand harsh northeastern winters as well as heavy rains and occasional overwatering.

The modern terrace and the facade of the building from the turn of the twentieth century complement each other, perhaps representing a design style becoming more popular as city dwellers seek to integrate old and new, outdoors and indoors at various levels of affordability and taste.

LEFT: Jay Johnson, designer of the apartment, comments on the extension of space that the garden brings to the interior, noting, "You have a beautiful view of nature from everywhere in the apartment."

OPPOSITE: There are ten trees on the terrace: eight heritage river birches and two white crape myrtles. Additional wooden planters contain smaller trees as well as grasses, shrubs, miniature boxwood, climbing hydrangea, and clematis.

PAGES 54—55: The rear of the peaked facade of the 1905 Renaissance revival building creates an interesting barrier wall on the west terrace. From the apartment there are views of tulips and daffodils in the spring with ligularia, begonias, and foxtail fern following in summer. Eucalyptus leaves and holly adorn the garden in the winter months.

A Rooftop Garden
with French Flair

A rooftop garden can be inviting almost all year round if it is beautiful and fun to be in. This terrace garden is a haven from New York, an unexpected touch of the South of France on the Upper East Side of Manhattan, and clearly reflects the ebullient personalities of the owners.

Boxwood hedges rise almost seven feet high to block intrusive views of buildings to the south. A stout aluminum chimney shoots a fifteen-foot diagonal above the west side of this garden, designed by Halsted Welles Associates, but it is hardly offensive covered as it is in trailing ivy.

A bistro-style setup just beyond the arched trellis entrance stands ready for drinks, and several seating areas beckon visitors to relax. Those in the mood for exercise can shoot balls into the basketball hoop near the kitchen door. Mid-terrace, a firebox is stocked with logs that will take the chill off the cool evening air, so the garden can be enjoyed at night and in seasons of the year other than summer.

Chaise longues and sofas upholstered in canvas with throw pillows covered in turquoise, jade, lavender, and pink suggest a nearby beach; however there is no ocean, only a stream of traffic running a steady course on the avenue many stories below.

LEFT: An archway with mandevilla and trellises covered in roses suggest that this is a garden in France. Flashes of red and pink are everywhere, in fuchsia, hibiscus, and New Guinea impatiens. Bamboo at the northeast corner and dwarf Alberta spruce complete a background of greenery.

RIGHT: There are no tall trees in this lush and verdant garden because of building code restrictions. Instead, height is achieved by the use of trellises and a wrought-iron fence covered in climbing vines. Dwarf Alberta spruces are permitted along the east-facing parapet. Sweet autumn clematis and Japanese holly hedges create a natural wall to the south.

LEFT: What more pleasant place could there be for a nap or a chat than this daybed overflowing with pillows coordinated with the colors of the garden? Roses cover the trellis, and bamboo and exotic grasses fill in the gaps with green.

BELOW: A basketball hoop is tucked under a bower of wisteria with a shower next to it for cooling off.

OPPOSITE: Roses in late May and early June grow alongside bright pink and red geraniums, flowering tobacco, impatiens, and bamboo. The informal mixture lends an air of naturalness to this sunny garden.

RIGHT: Le Bistrot de Fifi is a good place for the owners to relax or entertain guests. The area is festooned with wisteria, clematis, and roses. The paving is precast concrete pavers with a sandblasted finish.

A Showcase for
Nature and Art

The triplex penthouse was added atop a prewar building to the
specifications of the very imaginative owners, creating a multitiered
garden. The outdoor space reflects the owners' desire to engage
the classical elements of earth, water, air, and fire, in addition to
a fifth element called ether, which in Greek mythology referred
to the pure upper air that the gods breathed. Each of these elements
is represented in the garden in subtle ways and conceptually unifies
the design of the various spaces.

The planting in the garden is not complex. Boxwood in sturdy
containers and arborvitae, as well as two kinds of clumping bamboo,
provide a background of different shades of green. Spare furnishings
in natural wood are appealingly integrated and do not disturb the
peaceful mood. A wall of arborvitae with columns of English ivy
forms a protective barrier against urban noise and traffic below.
Nearby skyscrapers seem more decorative than obtrusive when viewed
from this secluded terrace.

RIGHT: Between the exterior glass walls of
the apartment and a tall hedge of evergreens
a path of white beach stones follows a trail
of lights to the summer dining area. An *ipe*
wood floor and a beige canopy that glows
with candlelight create an elegant garden
pavilion for multiseasonal use.

OPPOSITE: The outdoor eating area is illuminated by candlelight, nearby skyscrapers, and indirect light from inside the apartment. A carved wooden sculpture of Pinocchio by artist Jim Dine stands in the far corner of the living room.

BELOW: A mirror adjacent to the outdoor shower and a seating area reflects the serene garden of bamboo, boxwood, and evergreens.

LEFT: Neighboring skyscrapers do not intrude on the east-facing side of the terrace where sunlight and sky predominate.

OPPOSITE: Stainless steel chimneys manifest the owner's desire to represent the element of fire in her concept of a perfect garden. A skylight brings sun to the interior. Water from the outdoor shower offers relief from summer heat and alludes to one of the elements.

BELOW: Even in winter, this urban garden evokes a peaceful feeling and a quiet connection with nature. Under snow, the furniture becomes abstract sculpture for the apartment dwellers to contemplate from inside.

A Terrace of
Grand Proportions

First viewed through large, multipaned windows from inside the apartment, the 3,200 square feet of terrace was judiciously landscaped by Adele Mitchell so as not to be crowded by too much planting. Upon entering the garden, two rows of crabapple trees surrounded by coral-colored petunias and accommodated in massive pots draw one toward a grouping of arborvitae and blue spruce. These evergreens, flanked by a pair of limber pines, provide both privacy and year-round greenery.

The garden is glorious in spring with blooming rhododendron, Delaware Valley white azaleas, tulips, lush peonies, and pansies, followed in early June by displays of roses in pale pink (Heritage), almost coral pink (Abraham Darby), yellow (Graham Thomas), and an unusually splendid flourish of petal-pink hydrangea. These exuberant colors contrast with a background of white Himalayan birch and mature evergreens, including English boxwood and hinoki cypress ringed at the base with Willowleaf cotoneaster that displays tiny white flowers in spring and red berries in autumn. A kitchen garden of vegetables and herbs grows on the northeast side. Rhododendron flanked by kousa dogwood, all underplanted with white azaleas near weeping cutleaf Japanese maples, complete the concept of an established garden and ensure a pleasant view in seasons other than summer.

OPPOSITE: A landmarked building rooftop offers the perfect setting for an unusual garden terrace high above street level. On the northeast corner of the terrace near the kitchen garden, two kousa dogwoods offer a profusion of large white blossoms in late spring.

RIGHT: Petunias in shades of coral at the base of the crabapple trees provide a dash of color at the entrance to the garden. Directly ahead is a dense grouping of flowering shrubs and evergreens, ensuring year-round privacy.

BELOW: Steps from the apartment lead up to French doors that open onto the terrace where flanking rows of white flowering crabapple trees in large containers create a formal entrance to the large garden.

Curved seating areas form two ovals — one for cocktails, the other for dining — that are shaded by dark green awnings. On each side of the door onto the terrace stands a Katsura tree, which is deciduous with heart-shaped leaves. The terrace is paved with eighteen-inch-square pale terra cotta. A sturdy balustrade of brick and stone borders the terrace, with fenced openings offering visual continuity with the trees along Park Avenue below.

OPPOSITE: The furnishings in the cocktail area of the terrace are allowed to weather naturally. Even the massive plant containers spend winter out of doors. In summer the extended awnings create shady places to get away from the hot sun.

RIGHT: Between a pair of arborvitae a climbing yellow rose blooms all summer. In a blue ceramic container, a hydrangea boasts pink flowers that change in autumn to ivory with a rosy edge.

PAGES 78–79: The lush greens of the dwarf English boxwood and the Katsura trees, pruned to terrace proportions, are evident in the southern aspect of the garden. The patina of the furniture in the dining area is consistent with these natural shades. The roses, coral-pink petunias, and multicolored pansies provide a glorious splash of color.

Country Pleasures, Urban Views

The well-equipped garden terrace twelve stories above street level, created by interior designer Sheila Bridges with landscape architect Gresham Lang, has a decidedly lived-in look. Partial walls of cedar trellis visually protect the terrace, which is paved in rosy red-and-white patterned ceramic tiles. An opening in the trellis allows a breathtaking view of the Empire State Building, twenty blocks to the north.

Streamlined furniture in a synthetic weave, fortifying it against rain and intense sunlight, is supplemented by two long benches, each a carved trunk of Indonesian teakwood. Galvanized metal planters of varying heights painted dark brown overflow with a mixture of annuals, bulbs, and perennials, as well as aquatic plants, shrubs, trees, and vines. A four-inch-deep tray of succulents rests under the

RIGHT: Comfortable seating and a portable fireplace suggest an outdoor living room where one may enjoy cool breezes in summer with a spectacular view of the Empire State Building. A solar floor lamp provides a glow of light after sunset. Fragrant white moon-vine, yellow climbing rose, cardinal flower, clematis, and hydrangea combine to create a summer mood.

eave of a small penthouse bedroom adjacent to the terrace and is just barely visible from the inside. A similar tray with shade-tolerant perennials borders the north side of the bedroom on the outside. Above the planter three twelve-inch-deep shelves with an overhang of cedar trellis covered by wisteria provide a convenient place to mix drinks before dinner near the seating area on the north side.

OPPOSITE: Masses of summer plants — the foliage of white variegated dogwood, yellow coreopsis, purple violas, and weeping Japanese maples — add to the feeling of a country garden in the city. The cardinal flower attracts butterflies and hummingbirds.

BELOW: Fragrant plants, herbs, hydrangea, and vines extend the feeling of the country in summer with a cool backdrop of boxwood hedge.

OPPOSTE: Weeping Japanese maple underplanted with trailing white water hyssop, gray dichondra, and yellow creeping Jenny surrounding a figure of Buddha add an Asian note.

BELOW: Groupings of furniture of different types serve to define outdoor spaces meant for different uses: lounging, sunbathing, dining. Teak benches offer additional seating. The "rooms" may be viewed from the penthouse bedroom window looking toward the Hudson River and sunsets to the west.

A Romantic Retreat on the Upper East Side

In the right hands, a small outdoor space can become an elegant urban garden. Stepping into this Upper East Side garden one has, at first, the impression of reaching a clearing in a forest of oaks and evergreens that seems to enclose the space, but a closer look suggests that the garden beyond the living room is actually an extension of the interior. As the indoor furniture is spare and comfortable, the outdoor chairs of wrought iron and the table made by the owner of shaved pebbles pressed into resin are equally inviting. The color scheme, courtesy of the plants arranged neatly in sturdy boxes and containers, is mostly green and white: trailing ivy, small hostas, deadnettle, and vines of mandevilla and clematis that introduce a dash of brighter color here and there. Complementing the minimal color scheme are assorted succulents displayed as a table arrangement. In fall the colors change to a mix of rusts, yellows, and pinks from chrysanthemums and cyclamen.

LEFT: Glass doors open to create a seamless connection between the interior and the garden-terrace outside. Chairs made of wrought iron occupy very little visual space. The wall of the adjacent building offers protection to the garden on the western side as well as architectural interest.

"We worship the god of small spaces," declares the designer of the garden. She and her husband have furnished their cozy space with all that is necessary to enjoy a delicious meal en plein air. The wife—who through her business, Snap Décor, helps others to perform miracles similar to those demonstrated here—proclaims the joys of carefully choosing the objects with which one surrounds oneself. As a Californian, she never ceases to enjoy the pleasures of being in touch with nature, even in the middle of a metropolis, and caring for things that grow.

LEFT: Corners of the terrace are made particularly inviting with planters of tall upright arborvitae ringed by trailing ivy. The greenery can be enjoyed from the interior, seen from three doorways that open up from the living room.

OPPOSITE: Several styles of New York buildings form a pleasing backdrop for dining out of doors. Brick parapet walls lined with wooden planters support a birch tree for shade as well as a mix of hostas, ivy, and a variety of annuals.

PAGES 90–91: Viewed from the floor above, the terrace is a perfectly coordinated outdoor space. Planters along the sides are supplemented with window boxes mounted to the terrace railings. Variegated deadnettle (foreground) and vines of clematis and mandevilla add color in summer. Plants can be easily changed with the season.

ROOFTOP GARDEN as *Landscape*

A proper garden, ornamental or practical: for smelling roses or growing tomatoes

Classic and Modern Elements Mesh in a SoHo Garden

As neat and crisp as a well-tailored suit, this terrace garden reflects the attention to detail of its owner, who has a background in design and sculpture. The contemporary building by French architect Jean Nouvel stands in stunning contrast to its older, mostly cast-iron neighbors with arched windows and bold architectural details. It offers no clue to the surprise that awaits on the terrace of an apartment not even halfway up the building.

There is a seamless integration of interior and exterior space due to the floor-to-ceiling glass walls that separate the loftlike interior from the outdoor terrace. Once outside, the long lines of teak decking make the terrace seem endless. A tall hedge softens the far edge of the garden, which runs the length of the deck blocking out the tops of mostly mid-height buildings nearby. A pair of red Japanese maples at the east-facing side of the building and two smoke trees on the western side define each end of the terrace.

There are two shaded dining areas as well as chaise longues that can be moved to catch the sun. At night, boxes of light illuminate the

RIGHT: A ribbon of tulips bordering the longest side of the garden is a feature of the terrace in spring. These are followed in summer by roses, gardenias, and annuals in a medley of colors and fragrances.

terrace like paper lanterns, making dining outside a pleasure. On the southeast corner of the terrace a sail-like umbrella shades a swimming pool by day that is lit by an underwater light at night.

An outdoor shower like the one on this rooftop in downtown Manhattan could be called an eccentricity or the ultimate luxury. What greater

OPPOSITE: Rosebushes and an evergreen hedge frame a bed of spring flowers that includes tulips, hyacinths, and narcissus. In summer the roses are a cloud of pink.

RIGHT: Slender branches of red maple intermingle to form a perfect backdrop for the splash of color from masses of tulips in the foreground.

pleasure, after all, than showering, perhaps late at night, amidst the roses and gardenias of a summer garden in the city?

In fact, in summer, the garden becomes transformed with new plants and, sometimes, added lighting effects for a special occasion, suggesting the organic nature of modern design.

RIGHT: The position of the terrace on the seventh floor allows quiet enjoyment of the sunset in the evening and a rare view of decorative elements of nineteenth-century buildings nearby. Blue lights mounted to the spines of the umbrellas and additional lighting amongst the plantings produce a stunning effect for a special occasion.

BELOW: An unexpected feature of the terrace is the pool at the east corner, hardly obtrusive when it is covered and a tempting amenity when it is not. This pool is for serious exercise, with water jets providing a current to swim against in four feet of water.

Rural Elegance
High Above Central Park

This garden terrace by Halsted Welles Associates overlooking Central Park seems like a lofty extension of the park below. On a sunny day in April, daffodils are just giving way to blazing tulips; puffs of crabapple blossoms stand side by side with flowering cherry. Japanese maples are fully leafed out in early spring; climbing roses, hydrangea, and wisteria debut in a few weeks' time.

The garden is on two contrasting levels: the more spacious lower garden paved in quarry tile and perfect for entertaining is lush with colorful flowers and green Japanese maples that turn to shades of red and orange in the fall. The upper level suggests another world: the floor of the terrace is paved in flinty slate with accents of round stones in cool shades of blue and gray in the Japanese garden. This is a private area where the owners, both passionate gardeners, may

RIGHT: Spring flowers in bright colors coordinate with the red-toned quarry tile paving of the garden's lower level. A mass of green trees in Central Park forms the ideal background. The furniture, nineteenth-century French in style, has been refinished in a clear coating to preserve the silvery shade of the original wrought iron.

LEFT: A Japanese maple and a crabapple tree (right) frame this vignette of the New York skyline seen from the lower terrace.

OPPOSITE: A mixture of fiery-colored tulips makes a strong impression against a backdrop of azalea, rhododendron, blossoming crabapple, and Japanese tree lilac.

enjoy a salad of freshly picked vegetables from their rooftop garden at a quiet table in the corner with only the sound of a Japanese water fountain in the background.

There is a peaceful balance to the place as a whole. The juxtapositions of bright and subtle, evergreen and deciduous, rough and smooth, lend a feeling of perfect coordination. The skyline of the city viewed from here is the ultimate contrast to the serenity of this unusual retreat.

OPPOSITE: A bower of cast iron in an ivy-leaf pattern came with the apartment when the owners moved in. It provides shade from the sun and hides the parapet wall where planting could not conceal it. Roses in planters beyond signal a transition to an allée of dogwood and woodland flowers.

BELOW: On the upper terrace, English green slate sets the tone for a cooler palette of colors than that of the terrace below. Sargent's crabapple, High Hopes rosebushes, and a selection of specimen conifers blend in a background for tulips in purples and white.

LEFT: Bright green Japanese maple leaves and a bevy of daffodils bid a cheerful welcome to spring.

OPPOSITE: Because of stringent fire codes, the casement of the elevator bulkhead forming the left-hand wall of this Japanese garden was made from aluminum and painted to look like bamboo. Actual hardy bamboo mixes with red lace-leaf Japanese maples in the corner. Painted fiberglass "rocks" create a walkway surrounded by moss and beds of mondo grass.

A Place in the Sun

Wonderful things often come in small packages, as this 735-square-foot terrace makes abundantly clear. The clients requested a color scheme in shades of orange, yellow, and red, which led to the creation of this garden by Rush Jenkins and Klaus Baer of WRJ Design Associates, assisted by Gresham Lang of Gresham Lang Garden Design.

The specified colors blend in a mixture of shrub verbena, pale yellow roses, two varieties of Japanese maple, and red hibiscus, with accents of purple provided by lavender and salvia. The colors stand out against a background of the rich green of western red cedar nearly eight feet tall and planters packed with juniper, the lush, glossy foliage of a hardy gardenia, sage, and splashes of variegated Solomon's seal that enliven the mix with their lighter shade of green leaves tipped with white. A stand of butterfly bush rises high in one of the planters, attracting the attention of not only butterflies and hummingbirds in midsummer but also bees.

RIGHT: This open-air living room is fragrant with the scent of lavender and roses. The comfortable outdoor furniture was imported from France.

LEFT: Water hyssop complemented by silver-leafed hosta and variegated trailing foliage spills out of painted containers made of galvanized sheet metal.

OPPOSITE: The chairs are made of synthetic weave and are able to withstand the blazing sun. Three upright Japanese maples with coral bark stand along the south-facing parapet.

Well-designed planters serve to unify the robust garden, and these made of galvanized sheet metal painted in several coats of latex paint in precisely the right shade of butter yellow frame the garden and divide it into outdoor rooms for different purposes: socializing over cocktails, dining, and relaxing. The planters and plants provide a natural visual "wall" of separation between the different areas.

BELOW: A weeping red Japanese maple accents a mix of late-spring flowers including azaleas, tulips, lavender with silver foliage, hardy gardenias, and light red hibiscuses.

A Parklike Haven with Dramatic City Views

Approaching through a gate that suggests a medieval fortress within, one enters a cobblestone-paved, ivy-covered courtyard—the domain of what was formerly a metal foundry. The foundry went out of business in the 1940s, and the premises came to house many different small businesses. The current owners bought the property in 1979 and moved here in 1981. Much of the former foundry space has been extensively restored and renovated and is rented out for many purposes.

One reaches the family's headquarters via an industrial staircase that eventually opens onto a terrace comprised of squares of cast stone with a patch of river-polished stones surrounding a gigantic rusted wheel, a relic of the metal foundry. Now the wheel serves as a container for a small fountain and pool.

RIGHT: One of several seating areas on an expansive terrace, this grouping is created within borders of trees including quaking aspen and pines as well as plants that can be moved or changed with the season. The background of industrial facilities and the skyline of Manhattan form a striking contrast with the garden setting.

OPPOSITE: Variegated dogwood, weeping larch, wisteria, and red maple make this shady dining area inviting. Crocus and iris add color in spring, giving way to white mandevilla, Indian tobacco, and bright annuals in summer.

BELOW: Dwarf boxwood encircles a patio and cooling pond in this private corner of the garden where one may seek refuge on a hot summer day.

PAGE 118: Trees in large containers lend a feeling of permanency to a garden of many "rooms." What better place for a business meeting than this one where air-conditioning is not required?

PAGE 119: A cast-iron wheel makes an unusual container for a pool and quietly bubbling fountain tucked in amidst leafy papyrus. In late afternoon and evening the breathtaking view of the Queensboro Bridge and Manhattan beyond becomes the center of attention.

The garden has a slightly Asian feel due to the umbrellalike branches of a red Japanese maple that immediately catch the eye. However, many varieties of plants and trees live here and thrive in mammoth containers with automated irrigation. The variety is partly due to the fact that the owners once owned a landscaping business and they liked to rescue "orphans" that had been removed from clients' gardens because they had outgrown their space. A place can always be found here for one more plant to tuck in amongst the teakwood chairs and chaise longues, creating oases of breeze and shade and greenery that calm a busy mind. Views feature the Queensboro Bridge, the East River, and the Manhattan skyline—equally enthralling in daytime or at night.

A Gazebo Overlooks
Fifth Avenue

From this terrace one has a classic view across Central Park to the iconic buildings along the park's western border. Special areas of this rooftop garden, however, remain to be discovered closer at hand. On the west-facing side, low stone planters of the same material as the terrace paving form a verdant border without obscuring the breathtaking view. Two canopies of stone and steel provide welcome shade from the afternoon sun. Rhododendrons and a birch tree soften the corner where you turn southwest to a different zone of this multifaceted garden that was designed by Halsted Welles Associates. Past the corner, Japanese maple trees decorate a small area featuring a painted mural viewed from wrought-iron chairs under a pergola covered in wisteria.

The pathway narrows on the southeast side but doesn't end. Instead it opens to an east-facing view of city rooftops where comfortable chaise longues offer an opportunity for the owners to enjoy the sunrise. This terrace journey finishes at an artfully constructed gazebo at the northeast corner.

LEFT: This corner of the terrace garden, banked in flowers and vines, offers a true refuge from the frenzy of city life below. Here the owners may enjoy morning sun amidst mountain laurel, dogwood, mandevilla, and fragrant night-blooming moonflowers.

Like all terrace gardens, this one requires an elaborate watering system. The owner reports that one beautiful day she and her husband awoke to a call from the doorman reporting that it was raining in front of their building and people not expecting bad weather were complaining of getting wet. It took only a moment for the owners to realize that one of their watering pipes had sprung a leak, making a mockery of that morning's weather forecast.

OPPOSITE: The view to Central Park West features many classic landmarks including the Dakota, the triple towers of the Beresford, and the San Remo. The middle ground of trees changes with each season to provide a different colored background for entertaining on this terrace, decorated here with planters of spray roses.

BELOW: Cotoneaster and birch, as well as black and red chokeberries spilling out of planters, create an illusion of summer in the country, until one notices the Carlyle Hotel rising like an obelisk not far to the east.

RIGHT: The gazebo is built of lightweight aluminum and rests on steel outriggers. The whole assemblage is weighted down with planters filled with soil and plants including mountain laurel, snowdrift, skip laurels, red and black chokeberries, and climbing hydrangea.

BELOW: The maples are Tamukeyama Japanese maples, chosen for their color, echoing the rust tones in the mural.

Layers of Foliage on a Downtown Rooftop

These 1,500 square feet offer space for children to play safely as well as comfortable seating to enjoy a garden bursting with foliage and flowering plants. One level up, passing through a small grove of ivy and Japanese maples, the garden, designed by Halsted Welles Associates, opens again to a spacious area for cooking and dining outside. The view from this location in lower Manhattan seems at least 180 degrees wide, encompassing every style of building in New York history and featuring the Empire State Building approximately a mile away.

The flooring in the playground zone is made up of speckled squares of spongelike material to cushion bumped knees. Higher levels are covered in teakwood decking with furniture to match or complement. A perimeter hedge encloses the entire area, offering enough privacy to include an outdoor shower, in its own wooden enclosure, and another much larger structure housing an enormous water tank.

LEFT: This garden rests on a superstructure that extends across the roof with changes in level to designate areas designed for different purposes. Oakleaf and mophead hydrangeas mix with mountain laurel, boxleaf honey-suckle, and green Japanese maple to give the impression of a rustic retreat.

OPPOSITE: The leaves of a Chinese scholar tree wave delicately above the seating area. Boxleaf honeysuckle and sweet autumn clematis trail along the fencing that encloses one of several skylights transmitting light to rooms inside the apartment.

BELOW: In spring Japanese holly and Miss Kim lilac blossoms soften the edge between the private rooftop garden and city rooftops beyond.

LEFT: Plants with a variety of foliage — and intriguing names such as Henryana, Rubus and bugleweed — blend with more familiar Japanese maples and willow to create a thicket of green on several levels. To meet restrictions of weight on rooftops, the fountain is mounted to the brick wall.

An Oasis of Calm in TriBeCa

Above the maelstrom of traffic in and out of the Holland Tunnel there lies a forest of hydrangeas, birch trees, and weeping red maples. They spill out of ceramic pots and planters on a deck that may be the only oasis of calm in a busy district of former warehouses in New York's TriBeCa neighborhood. The deck, supporting the display of plants laid out by Plant Specialists, is of composite flooring the color of milk chocolate. Hurricane lanterns of filigreed ironwork add soft light after dark. The deck turns a corner on the northeast elevation, though not exactly at a right angle, as the familiar grid of Manhattan becomes a cobweb in this part of town.

The luxuriant blooms of white hydrangea are first viewed through large windows from a generously proportioned dining room. From here the terrace is a visual extension of the interior, designed by

LEFT: A comfortable seating arrangement suggests an outdoor living room decorated with red maples, gold-tipped arborvitae, and hydrangeas. The furniture is made of weatherproof synthetic resin. Individual hurricane lamps supplement low-voltage electric lighting at night.

Thomas Jayne Studio. Outside, there are two main dining areas: one is furnished to accommodate a group of six or eight; further on, closer to the apartment kitchen, there is a second area with a round table ideal for breakfast in the early morning sun.

Level changes between one dining area and another help to emphasize the shift from an informal area to one perfect for entertaining a larger

RIGHT: Light and sunshine pour in through multipaned windows that suggest a country house set in the middle of a garden. The table and chairs to the right create an area perfect for afternoon tea.

BELOW: Masses of pompoms, gold-tipped arborvitae, and hydrangeas line the approach to the outdoor living room in this lushly planted rooftop garden.

group. Finally, outside the bedroom on the north side of the building the level changes again, like a stage set, denoting the most private area where two lounge chairs invite the owners to enjoy a few quiet moments when, perhaps, no guests are expected.

OPPOSITE: Pompoms and juniper flank the dramatic entrance to this spacious garden. Despite its impressiveness, this garden is not complex and is easy to maintain. The hydrangeas last until winter and the evergreens all year long. Only fernspray hinoki among the hydrangeas might need to be replaced in the spring.

RIGHT: A favorite place for breakfast in warm weather features furniture that is made of hand-cast aluminum with an electrically sprayed powder coating, a process that ensures durability in outdoor conditions.

Outdoor Entertaining, Day and Night

In this sleek, soberly modernist building there are many references to nature in a distinctive architectural setting. The theme is continued on the terraces adjoining an opulent duplex apartment on the east side of the highest floor in the building.

The garden by Halsted Welles Associates reveals itself in stages depending on the season. In early spring its ornaments convey a sense of antiquity: a Roman fountain run dry, a chunk of masonry seemingly kicked aside for the time being, an antique mirror clouded with age. The perennials are still covered to protect them from stormy blasts. In spring and early summer rhododendrons, pink and white roses, and hydrangeas abound. The fountain is filled with succulents in shades of purple and green. The architectural artifact is propped in place. The mirror, cleaned and shined, reflects the stately towers of upper Manhattan.

RIGHT: Bar Harbor junipers planted in simulated limestone appear to be growing from deep within the parapet wall. Eastern red cedars frame the area where Annabelle hydrangeas thrive in summer.

Though this is a rooftop terrace on three sides of the building, one has a feeling of meandering as one passes through a stone archway to the east garden, not knowing what to expect. Upon exploration, several areas seem perfect for entertaining, whether a tea party or a formal dinner.

Up another level, rhododendron, yew, weeping cherry, bayberry, juniper, and evergreen trees suggest a forest retreat somewhere far from Manhattan. This is a favorite place for open-air dining, where tables, chairs, and cushions can be set up at a moment's notice.

OPPOSITE: Roses and honeysuckle climb the lattice in late spring, framing not a window but a reflected view of neighboring skyscrapers and potted white phalaenopsis orchids on the table in front of the mirror.

RIGHT: The container filled with succulents is a cast-fiberglass replica of a terra-cotta antique and is able to withstand harsh weather conditions.

LEFT: A previous owner of the
penthouse—Charlie Chaplin's
widow, Oona O'Neill—wanted
an open pergola where roses
could grow without blocking the
sun. The current owners are
the beneficiaries. The rose garden
is underplanted with catmint.

ROOFTOP GARDEN as *Aerie*

A perch above the teeming city, the sky within reach

Endless Views from Olympian Heights

Manhattan's Time Warner Center—its two towers soaring skyward— seems an unlikely location for a residential terrace. Even close scrutiny of the towers does not reveal this unlikely architectural feature. On the seventy-sixth floor of the north tower, however, there is a setback accommodating what must be the city's highest garden. No buildings—near or far—block the astounding views: north to the George Washington Bridge, east to Long Island, and on a clear day even as far as Connecticut.

The 1,200-square-foot terrace, designed by Carlos Aparicio of Aparicio + Associates, has a reassuringly robust parapet with glass panels through which one may view the spectacular surroundings. Aristide Maillol's bronze nude *L'Air* reclines near the western end of the terrace, as if languishing nonchalantly in a private garden.

LEFT: The extraordinary vantage point offers incomparable views of Manhattan, the Hudson River, and New Jersey. At this height, it can be windy on the terrace, and plants must be chosen that are compatible with the often harsh conditions. Additionally, the furniture is securely fastened to the terrace floor to resist being blown away by gusts of wind.

The sculpture is perfectly aligned with the entrance to the apartment, serving as an invitation to see the city from this staggering height. The terrace is visually experienced from both levels of the 6,511-square-foot duplex—through the floor-to-ceiling glass walls of the main floor and from the windows in the floor above. The lighting and sound system, designed by the architect, are unobtrusive and create an atmosphere of informal refinement.

RIGHT: Maillol's *L'Air* (1938) seems at home above the rooftops of Manhattan. Glass panels in the parapet wall permit unsurpassed views from the lounging and dining areas.

BELOW: Climbing hydrangea and lavender combine with trailing pine and plum yew in shades of green and purple. The border planter below contains a mix of stonecrops and sempervivum, often called "hen and chicks."

The team of landscape designers, Gresham Lang and Kevin Wegner, assisted the architect in the garden layout that included minimal plantings that could tolerate the microclimate zone on the terrace.

OPPOSITE: The view to the east offers a panorama of well-known New York skyscrapers including Citigroup Center with its wedge-shaped roof easily seen in the distance.

RIGHT: Custom-designed metal planters match the bronze cladding of the parapet. Plantings of blue juniper, yellow coreopsis, blue spruce, and grasses complete the effect of an established container garden. The flooring is made from grooved concrete pavers.

Graceful Garden Living Above Park Avenue

This apartment is legendary, having once been owned by Gianni Agnelli of Fiat and his stylish wife, Marella. But the building is distinctive for other reasons. It is one of many buildings built in 1929 before the Great Depression, and it benefited from the multiple-dwelling law passed in that year that allowed apartment buildings to rise to nineteen stories provided the top floors were set back. The result in this building and its twin across the street is an unusual arrangement of penthouses, duplexes, and triplexes, with windows designed to take advantage of views in several directions.

Another feature that followed the unconventional angling of apartments above the twelfth floor was the possibility of having small gardens in unlikely places. In this apartment, for example, the visitor faces a mini garden with a Roman fountain and wall sculpture

LEFT: Red maple foliage, a specimen hinoki cypress, and a border of blue hydrangeas accent an unusual view of a post-1929 building in which setback floors created opportunities for terraces.

immediately upon stepping out of the elevator. It is tucked beneath what appears to be a flying buttress, an architectural element supporting the structure above. Another mini garden, on what might be more accurately described as a balcony rather than a terrace, adjoins the living room. Both gardens feature spreading red maples, ivy, and boxwood hedges supplemented by hydrangeas and pansies in summer with seasonal plantings at other times of the year.

RIGHT: Stone paving provides a contrast with brightly colored foliage and blooms along the east wall of the terrace. A boxwood hedge softens the edge overlooking an assortment of buildings in various architectural styles.

OPPOSITE: From a second smaller terrace adjoining the apartment one views the larger one facing north and east.

RIGHT: Glass doors from the living room open onto the narrower end of the terrace. Climbing hydrangea decorates the wall where the terrace extends northward under an archway to the opposite end.

A Breathtaking Panorama from Central Park West

The terrace and garden, designed by Barbara Britton, is approached by a stairway leading from the apartment to a conservatory added to the building in 1987. From the terrace a breathtaking panorama of Central Park and the New York skyline unfolds, extending from West 57th Street to the south to beyond the reservoir and the north end of the park. The east-facing iron railing presents no impediment to the view and is minimally decorated with a border of Silver King Japanese spindle tree, a deciduous plant native to East Asia. A narrower version of the south and west aspects of the rooftop terrace exists on the floor below, not far from the apartment kitchen and convenient for outdoor dining.

RIGHT: The essence of Manhattan seems laid out in this view facing east across the treetops of Central Park. The lawn is an unexpected feature at this level. Silver King Japanese spindle tree, a broad-leafed evergreen with flowers in yellow and green shades, has pinkish-red berries favored by many species of birds. A red weeping Japanese maple and a sphere of boxwood provide contrast in color and form near the lounge chairs.

The green expanse of Central Park is echoed in a lawn on the upper terrace that appears to be planted directly on the roof surface but is, in fact, contained in an ingenious system of square modules. The lawn extends from the base of an ivy-covered Italianate structure, which conceals the building's water tower and provides useful storage space for the lawn mower and garden tools.

OPPOSITE: The terrace is accessed from the conservatory. From this glass-walled room, one gets a preview of the panorama of architecture and the delights of this urban garden high above Central Park.

BELOW: Matching the material of the lime-stone coping and the stylized pineapple ornaments are rectangular containers planted with annuals that are rotated seasonally.

LEFT: Approximately seven hundred feet square, the lawn is comprised of four-foot-square modules, identical to those used at the tennis courts at Wimbledon, the Beijing National Stadium built for the 2008 Summer Olympics, and many American football stadiums.

From this urban aerie, several features of Central Park are discernible, such as Belvedere Castle and the Great Lawn, as well as the rooftops of the buildings comprising the Metropolitan Museum of Art. The terrace continues along the south side of the building to a large, open yet private space, affording views of the pinnacles of some of Manhattan's most distinguished residential buildings.

RIGHT: On the west-facing terrace, a privacy screen was created with a mix of conifers, broad-leaved evergreens, and coniferous shrubs including cypress, Alberta spruce, and juniper as well as variegated Japanese spindle trees and hydrangeas.

Elegance
in the Clouds

A house in the country may be expected to ramble from room to room, offering pleasing glimpses of lawn and garden here and there. But when that house is a duplex penthouse eighteen floors above street level, these views come as a stunning surprise.

The formal dining room, decorated in the neoclassical style of France under Louis XVI, is complemented by a more intimate dining area with floor-to-ceiling glass windows and doors. The doors can be opened in temperate weather for the diners to enjoy the climbing hydrangea, espaliered pear trees, and wisteria.

Most surprising perhaps is the miniature lawn outside the dining room. Even though the grassy lawns of Central Park far below might occasionally seem parched with thirst, this one stays lush and green from two waterings per day.

OPPOSITE: Trailing Boston ivy, cascading over the parapet wall, and climbing roses meet to form a pleasing backdrop for dwarf evergreens and English boxwood on the terrace below. A Japanese black pine thrives near the corner of the downstairs terrace.

Another garden on the second floor faces north, and in early June as well as late August into early fall it is replete with yellow roses and jasmine. A small third terrace outside the master bedroom overlooks Central Park and is further enhanced by its own tiny garden. The small gardens upstairs in this elegant penthouse are part of a progression from the downstairs area where guests are frequently entertained to the more private spaces above. The gardens, in all their permutations, reflect the creativity of the owner.

LEFT: A plumbago tree with lavender flowers occupies the corner of the family's sunny, informal dining room, which opens onto a small lawn many levels above Central Park.

OPPOSITE: The dining room doors may be opened in warm weather for a breezy view of espaliered pear trees, tree-form wisteria, and climbing hydrangea mingled with Boston ivy. Or, one may relax outside on a carpet of real grass.

OPPOSITE: Facing west across Central Park, the miniature lawn seems to meet the treetops in a blend of summer greens. Pear trees, cosmos, and leafy annuals complete the idyllic picture.

BELOW: This small terrace adjoining the master bedroom is a good place for coffee under the mid-morning sun. Oleander trees in antique planters carved from lava draw the eye to the view toward Central Park South.

A Sculpture Park
in the Sky

This distinctive penthouse occupies the full rooftop of an elegant building on Sutton Place. Upon entering the apartment one steps into crisp, white interiors that look out onto surrounding terraces. The rooms of this apartment house a collection of exciting twentieth-century art that extends onto the terrace garden designed by Ken Smith. Plantings are minimal. Works of art create the ornamentation. Prominently displayed on the west terrace is an oversize sculpture of a green diamond ring by Jeff Koons. Adjacent to this piece is an installation by Ken Smith of single artificial flowers projecting horizontally out of the white-painted brick wall.

Planters in several locations contain greenery that can be seen from inside. The terrace narrows as it winds around to the east following the lines of the building. The outdoor space encircles the apartment, allowing one to wander with the aim of seeing impressive urban views, enjoying the sun, or viewing some well-known contemporary art.

RIGHT: The view of Roosevelt Island and the Queensboro Bridge to the northeast is framed by two sculptures by Murakami, which may represent the roles of either sentinels or traditional topiaries.

LEFT: *Green Diamond* (2004) by Jeff Koons commands the apartment's west terrace. On this stark terrace, the color of the sculpture could allude to traditional garden greenery.

BELOW: Coniferous bushes are housed in a cubist formation of containers. Sweeping views that include the Queensboro Bridge can be seen from this vantage point.

LEFT: The terrace and garden are an understated work of art in and of themselves, not only for the plantings and the art but also for the views that they afford. Ken Smith, designer of the terrace, constructed an installation called *Flowers* that, like the other artwork in the space, plays with traditional garden precepts.

Above the Treetops
of Central Park

Not only way above the treetops but above the flight patterns of most birds, this terrace garden by Miguel Pons Landscaping offers spectacular views of old and new architectural landmarks on the south and west sides of Central Park. The San Remo is there, almost directly across the park, and on either side one can see the Beresford, the towers of the Time Warner Center, and the gemlike Hearst Tower.

This view determined the design and nature of the garden terrace. The owners decided against a flower garden and chose instead to frame their view of Central Park by picking up the colors of the park with low-growing perennials and annuals, letting them come together in a tapestry of greens, yellows, and maroons.

RIGHT: The plants on the narrow west-facing terrace are a medley of dwarf cypresses, Hina cedar, and annuals such as strawberry firetail and red cat's tail that bloom all summer. Kingswood Gold and Japanese forest grass with pale purple and soft green succulents are mixed in. Near the door to the terrace is a dwarf Colorado spruce underplanted with alumroot.

The journey along the terrace takes one past birches at each corner to an extension of the garden on the east side of the building where a bowl of mixed plants like the ones in the larger area creates a centerpiece in a small space.

OPPOSITE: From the dining room inside, or at the table on the terrace, the residents of the apartment have a view across the treetops of Central Park to the stately towers of the Upper West Side.

BELOW: Trellises at both ends of the west-facing terrace made of wire stretched across wooden frames are covered in crimson pygmy barberry, which produces a yellow bloom in May. Combined with this vine is Mohave firethorn, which flowers in May and produces red berries in autumn.

Low, white lightweight fiberglass bowls of various diameters and eighteen-inch-high copper planters are the containers of choice for this garden, creating an effect of pleasing uniformity. Someday the coppery color of the long planters may change to green due to long-term oxidation—like the reverse of the annual seasonal change of the trees in the park below.

RIGHT: A birch tree marks the corner of the terrace at the southeast end of the building. The large bowl contains a mixture including blue agave, honeyflower, Empress candle plant, and Kingswood Gold Jewels of Opar. The smaller bowls overflow with stonecrop, shell ginger, leopard plant, and elephant ear.

BELOW: An abstract sculpture by Joel Shapiro is part of the owners' collection of work mainly by contemporary artists.

BELOW: The terrace offers a panoramic view of New York architecture that could be called unmatched. Extending along Central Park West from Columbus Circle to West 90th Street, it includes a mix of early-twentieth-century buildings, such as the San Remo and the Beresford, as well as the Time Warner Center, finished in 2004.

Garden Designers

Adele Mitchell Inc.
Landscape design and architecture
315 East 65th Street
New York, NY 10065
greensleevesgardensltd@verizon.net
212 794 0390
540 454 5554 (Virginia)

Barbara Britton
Garden design and consulting
New York, NY
bbritton212@earthlink.net
212 799 0711

Gresham Lang Garden Design, LLC
135 Fifth Avenue, 2nd Floor
New York, NY 10010
greshamlanggardens.com
info@greshamlanggardens.com
212 598 1151

Halsted Welles Associates, Inc.
287 East Houston Street
New York, NY 10002
hwa@halstedwelles.com
212 777 5440

Miguel Pons Landscaping, LLC
130 West 30th Street, #16B
New York, NY 10001
miguelponslandscaping.com
mapons0210@aol.com
212 255 6310

Paula Hayes
510 East 13th Street
New York, NY 10009
paulahayes.com
info@paulahayes.com
212 420 7733

Plant Specialists
42-25 Vernon Boulevard
Long Island City, NY 11101
plantspecialists.com
sales@plantspecialists.com
718 392 9404

Rebecca Cole GROWs
214 West 30th Street
New York, NY 10001
rebeccacolegrows.com
info@rebeccacolegrows.com
212 216 9492

Snap Décor
Marjorie Reed Gordon
marjalago@aol.com
212 933 1131

Studio Gerard Landscape Architecture
18 Park Place
Brooklyn, NY 11217
kevingerard@mindspring.com
718 399 6998

Thomas Hays Interiors
248 West 23rd Street, Penthouse
New York, NY 10011
thomashaysinteriors.com
thays@thomashaysinteriors.com
212 741 8548

WORKSHOP:
Ken Smith Landscape Architect
79 Chambers Street, 2nd Floor
New York, NY 10007
212 791 3595

WRJ Design Associates, LLC
15 Broad Street, Suite 3230
New York, NY 10005
wrjassociates.com
info@wrjassociates.com
212 742 1623

Acknowledgments

The allure of private outdoor space, especially in an urban context, is powerful, and the task of maintaining these gardens in New York City can be complicated but most rewarding. The process of locating and editing the selection of gardens for this book was challenging, but the journey was interesting, entertaining, and ultimately inspiring.

We express our heartfelt thanks to the many wonderful people who helped us bring this book to fruition. We are so grateful to the loyal team who encouraged us to create a book featuring some of the most beautiful private outdoor spaces in New York City.

We are grateful to Marianne Strong, our literary agent, and her assistant Diana Oswald for all they have done to make our book proposal a reality.

The Rizzoli family has been our guiding light. We thank our publisher Charles Miers for his encouragement and support from the beginning. Our editor Philip Reeser has worked tirelessly 24/7 to make this book a collection of some of the most beautiful rooftop gardens. Our thanks go to Jane Newman, who immediately said yes to our idea and helped us move this project forward.

With the talent of Norman McGrath, an exceptional photographer, we were able to capture the beauty of each space. Molly McGrath was instrumental in collecting pertinent facts and stories about the history of each garden and how they are used today. Victoria Pohlmann has taken the material and designed a beautiful book.

We thank all the owners who let us into their private residences and shared their secret gardens with us. The landscape designers, gardeners, and architects who are responsible for creating many of these amazing spaces were generous in sharing their time and information with us. Their talents are evident throughout the book.

Evelyn Lauder's foreword and Dominique Browning's introduction set the stage for the visual delights that the reader will encounter while turning the pages of *Rooftop Gardens*.

And, finally, we thank both of our wonderful families and dear friends for all their encouragement, patience, and support while we were so focused on working on this book.

Denise LeFrak Calicchio
Roberta Model Amon

Photographer's Note

All photographs for this book were taken during 2010 using Canon equipment. My camera was the EOS 5D Mark II digital single-lens reflex with a 21.1 megapixel CMOS sensor. This provided RAW files sufficiently large to withstand considerable cropping without compromise. I used the following lenses—24mm $f/3.5$ Tilt/Shift Mark II, 17mm $f/4.0$ Tilt/Shift, 24-105mm $f/4.0$ IS, zoom, and 70-200mm $f/2.8$ zoom. A Speedlite 580EX II and a Speedlite 270EX provided fill light when needed. A Slik tripod provided support. Except for night views I set my camera at 200 ISO in manual mode. For most shots, except close-ups, I used an aperture of $f/8.0$. Finally, images were tweaked and adjusted as necessary in Adobe Photoshop on a Mac computer.

Norman McGrath

Colophon

This book was typeset in Mrs. Eaves, designed by Zuzana Licko in 1996 and licensed by the Emigre type foundry. The font is based on the work of the eighteenth-century English printer and typographer John Baskerville, and it is named for his assistant, who eventually became his wife after the death of Mr. Eaves.